This book is dedicated to my wife - my partner, my friend.

Copyright © 2017 by Mezen, INC

ISBN: 978 15455 16089

All rights reserved, including the rights to reproduce this book or portions thereof in any form whatsoever.

For information contact

Mezen, INC 8268 Davis Street, Minneapolis, MN 55357 USA

MEZEN, INC

Table of Contents

Chapter ONE – America is still the BEST place to earn a living	page 4
Chapter TWO – Make a decision – are you truly in sales?	page 8
Chapter THREE – Who influences you?	page 15
Chapter FOUR – Understand sales resistance and how to lower it	page 21
Chapter FIVE – Strengthen your sales muscles	page 28
Chapter SIX – Be a hunter – Run circles around your competition	page 34
Chapter SEVEN – Be a farmer – Run circles around your competition	page 42
Chapter EIGHT – 7 ½ Ways to promotion	page 50
Chapter NINE – 5 Ways to a pay raise	page 58
Chapter TEN – Get your sales career on track	page 63
Final Thoughts on Becoming a Stone-cold Seller	page 68
About the Author	page 71

AMERICA IS STILL THE BEST PLACE TO EARN A LIVING!

CHAPTER 1

On a recent business trip from Salt Lake City, I was flying next to a gentlemen from France. We got talking and I found out he was doing business in the US and came here every other month for a couple of weeks at a time.

He spoke a little about what he does and then I asked him a question,

"How do you like doing business in America?"

"Oh I like it a lot" he answered.

"It is very easy doing business in America" he said with his French accent.

He started counting on his fingers.

"The American people have good work ethic – they are hard-working, they are true to their word – they are reliable and they have customer service focus" he rattled those things out. I wanted to know more so I asked him "How is doing business in America different from Europe?"

"Well, in America you are less strategic and more implementation oriented. I mean in Europe people would strategize, argue about things and have great debates about business, then nothing gets done. You are better implementers."

We exchanged some other pleasantries, and as I sat back I began processing what I just heard. I grew up in Europe, if you can call Russia - Europe, more like Eurasia, really. But, I knew exactly what he was talking about. It's just that after twenty-five years in the States, I had begun to forget about that.

I grew up hustling on the streets of Leningrad in the former Soviet Union. The funny thing is most of the younger people, most likely don't even know what it was and where it was. Everything about the place I grew up is messed up. I mean, it's bad enough the city I grew in changed names after I left, from Leningrad to St. Petersburgh. The whole damned country changed names as well, from Soviet Union to Russian Federation. You've got to admit it, this is pretty messed up. Since the age of fourteen I explored opportunities to improve my financial status. In Soviet Union, communism was everywhere around me, because of this he hustle was not easy. As a matter of fact, it was illegal and dangerous to your health to do what I did. But more about it later.

From its first days, America has been built on progress, and moving forward is essential to execution and implementation. Right? If you arrived on the boat back in 1600s there was no welcome party to meet you and you had to build your own place to live. You had to stop strategizing and just built a dwelling. Then when you wanted to eat, you could not wait till someone brought you food and since there were probably very few restaurants and grocery stores back then you had to grow your own food.

My wife and I came to this country twenty-six years ago (legally) with $50 in our pockets and two half-filled suitcases. Let me tell you I was blessed to have a welcome party of strangers who let us live with them and fed us well. Couple of months of that and we were on our own. We fought and clawed through poverty and finally made it. I mean, I'm not a millionaire, yet, but if you average my income over the last twelve years (I made six figures every year and it has been improving every year), I earned close to two. Hey, I'm not bragging, but if a Russian can do it, then anyone CAN.

If you woke up today in the good old U. S of A, you are one of the most fortunate people on the planet earth. There is no excuse you must be able to make it! As Larry Wingett says it *"your success is your own damn fault"*. Your odds are so much better off if you woke up here versus Afghanistan or Spain.

So what's that got to do with sales? It has everything to do with sales. America is the greatest environment for sales, no matter whether you sell tangibles or intangibles. Whether it is Business to Business or Business to Consumer, you are a winner from the start. The problem is, most sales people think it is hard to earn money and make a living. They drag themselves going to work and complain endlessly about their commissions. Well, figure this out, you are sitting on a gold mine.

If you are in sales and are not getting the results you want, WAKE UP! Stop blaming your environment. *It's not selling season. Economy is still struggling. I get bad leads.* Stop whining! People are always buying, businesses are always spending money, they just not spending it with you. You simply need to figure out how to get your share!

What are you afraid of? If you call and they say no? Or when you ask them for the order and they say no? Really? You are afraid of someone stopping you? Ask yourself this, *am I in charge of my sales destiny?* The answer must always be YES! This is America!

This country gave me, an immigrant from the Communist world, every opportunity to grow and prosper. It is one of the reasons I want to influence as many people as I possibly can. This is the reason I'm wrote this book.

In the next few chapters you will learn how to become a stone-called seller. As you read and learn, think of what becoming better at your trade will make of you in the process. Envision yourself becoming a great closer. Stretch your comfort zone and see how applying those ideas and approaches will help you bulletproof your sales career and improve your results.

To get the most out of this little book, after each chapter take a moment and jot down your thoughts, ideas and takeaways. Most importantly, take time to write down what you will start and what you will stop doing. Use this as your action plan to improve your sales skills and your outcomes.

MY TAKEAWAYS:

I will start _____

_____
_____
_____
_____
_____
_____
_____
_____
_____

I will stop _____

_____
_____
_____
_____
_____
_____
_____
_____
_____
_____

ARE YOU TRULY IN SALES?

CHAPTER 2

Let's talk about your career. Young people! Millennials! Gen Y! Old(er) people! Is career in sales for you? Hey, that's not a generational question, it is an individual question. Actually there are couple of questions - number one, **do you want to be in sales?** If you are reading this, most likely you are in sales or have some interest in sales career.

There are over 80 millions of young adults under 35 in the United States. With sales jobs in abundance it might be a great choice for you. But before you rush off and fill out applications and get into the world of sales, you may want to consider the second question – *is sales profession for you?*

Being in sales does not mean you are a good fit for the job. I have met and trained thousands of sales people. When it came to producing results, less than 10% of them were superstars. Majority were good. And there were quite a few that I could tell did not fit into a sales job. They were nice people and good employees, but at the end of the month they were not producers. Many of them struggled with the demands of a sales career.

Let's cover the Cons and Pros of getting into the world of sales. You are young and ambitious and you want to succeed. But you may be feeling stuck in an hourly or salaried position and considering getting into sales. Let's start with a few CONS. Sorry for being negative off the bet. But, here are the things to consider before you apply for a sales position.

THE CONS: Number one – no guaranties.

When you get into sales, in most cases you have to generate your own book of business. Very few jobs offer you a list of clients that you can farm for business right away and get paid. In most commission-based jobs you eat what you kill. You generate your own leads; you generate your own sales. And it can take a while to learn all the ins and outs of the business.

I'm most familiar with auto sales. In my 14 years in car sales, I have seen a handful of folks who never sold cars before and in the first month generated huge paychecks. This is simply not common. Again, for majority of people, whether you get into car sales, real estate or any other high ticket sales it could take a while to get going. I can tell you I met hundreds of sales people who were so excited coming off the shoot, having great plans of making $100K right away, only to find out this was difficult and takes more work than they expected.

You can make $100K plus per year in sales. There is no denial, people do it all the time, it just takes longer than you expect and most people give up before they get there. Depending on the job, some sales transactions take months, even years. Since I left the car business and went into Business to Business sales, my average deal takes six months. There just so much more going on than a customer simply picking a color or the trim level of a new pickup truck.

When you are young you may not have too many financial commitments yet. It might work out for you to buckle up and wait for results during your first few months.

So, be prepared – as my friend says, **everything takes twice as long as you think it will.**

In addition to all of this, your schedule can be chaotic. Sales, especially retail sales can be demanding. The amount of time you spend getting your business going can be equal to your minimum wage or below. You can be working nights or mornings or all day every day. You can be working weekends. This might not work if you like social time with your friends. Since you can be working weird hours, you must seriously consider this. **Is it worth getting into?** You got to ask yourself these questions: **Are you better off finding a stable job with a guaranteed pay? Is hourly pay or salaried pay better for you?** Well, it might be. Unless of course you want to grow financially and get greater rewards.

THE CONS: Number Two – rejections.

Look sales world is full of them. People tell you *no* all the time! Get used to it. If you have a thin skin you, will not make it. You can only fake it for so long. It will get to you.

You have to roll with punches. Know that getting punched or grinded by your prospective buyers is very common – not physically of course. You will put your heart and soul into preparing for you prospect. You will spend time. You will wait. And they do not show up. Or they call the meeting off. At times you will go all the way and think you have the deal. You call your realtor. You book a trip to Hawaii. AND then – they tell you *no,* they went with a competitor. It is simply the reality of the sales world. So don't book a trip or call your realtor. If you cannot handle people un-friending you on Facebook, you will not make it. If you simply don't care about this, you will be ok. Your skin must and will get thicker.

Let's get positive! Here are the PROS for going into sales.

PROS: Number One – You can earn $100k in sales.

66% of Americans earn less than $42K and the average household earns $50K. Just google this. So, if earning the amount twice as average amount does not motivate you to go into sales I'm not sure what will. I guess if you are already earning more than that then I get it.

Listen, just because you have that potential does not mean you will earn it. (Here I go negative again). As a matter of fact, if sales was easy everyone would do it. **Sales is not easy, but it is not complicated.** You don't have to have a degree in rocket science to do it. You do have to have a degree in people science. There are multiple ways to earn high income in sales but the point is you CAN do it, and you should do it PERIOD. By the way, this is the only time I will tell you should do something.

YOU SHOULD EARN $100K PLUS! **Why?** This is yours to answer.

PROS: Number Two – sales will make you a stronger person.

Now I do not mean this physically, although in some retail jobs physical stamina is helpful. Sales will make you a stronger person in the following areas –

- people/relationships skills,
- communication skills,
- patience,
- tenacity,
- planning and organizational skills.

There are a ton of what people call soft skills that you can learn that will be great for you in your future jobs, should you decide to move out of sales. Although in most professions out there, you will be involved with some form of sales aspect. Listen, I was in an optometrist office – an eye doctor. From the moment I walked in, it was a one long sales pitch. I encountered four people including an eye doctor and all four were selling me on something. And this is eye doctor's office, right? Since I'm a sales trainer I'm more in-tune when someone is pitching me, even when they do it softly. Most people don't notice this, I do. Back in the office when they told me I have 20/20 vision they still had something to offer me – blank glasses or sunglasses. Those ladies had their pitches down. They were smooth and relentless. So sales skills will make you a stronger individual all around.

Many of these skills will make you more disciplined and much more prepared to face life, no matter what you decide to do in your life. I would go as far as to tell you that, in my humble opinion, everyone must experience sales world and live on commissions.

PROS: Number three – it's rewarding.

The biggest satisfactions I got over the years from sales jobs was the fact that it allowed me to win a lot. I love to win. I mean, I hate losing so that means that I love to win. I want to be on the top of whatever I do. This is by far the biggest motivator for me.

Now I get it, this is my values and my motivator, but I can tell you I met a lot of top performing sales people and they could tell you that money is the result of their passion for winning. As one millionaire client of mine said – ***money is secondary.*** My personal mission is to influence as many people as I possibly can. Bringing massive amounts of value to your clients and partners is what you want to focus on. When you do this sales become the most rewarding profession. And money will come. Keep you focus on solving your customer's problems.

You got to know yourself. If you have some form of ADD, cannot stand monotonous activities, like to meet different people, don't mind being blown-off by those people, ready for a challenge, eager to learn and earn, then sales profession is worth your attention. This can be super rewarding.

My final advice would be – ***stick with it.*** I took me a couple of years to finally realize that this is my career, because I thought it would be temporary for me, I did not apply myself 100 %. When I changed that attitude everything around me changed. Make a decision to have both feet firmly planted in your career, once you do, you will see a huge improvement in your performance.

Here is the recap:

Ask yourself these two questions:

- Do I want to be in sales?
- Is sales really for me?

The CONS:

- There are no guarantees in sales
- There are plenty of rejections

The PROS:

- You can make a great living
- It will make you a stronger individual
- It is super rewarding

MY TAKEAWAYS:

I will start _____

_____
_____
_____
_____
_____
_____
_____
_____
_____
_____

I will stop _____

_____
_____
_____
_____
_____
_____
_____
_____
_____
_____
_____

WHO INFLUENCES YOU?

CHAPTER 3

Your parents may have told you - *"stay away from bad influence."* I'm sure at some point of your adolescence you heard that advise. My dad told me that in the Soviet Union, so it works cross cultures. I think someone once said *"bad bla-bla-bla corrupts minds."* This is so true. Who are you talking to? Who are you listening to? Who are you associating yourself with? These are some real important questions. Look there is another saying that I found to be the rule almost like a law - *"you become the average of five people you associate yourself with."*

Remember the High School years? Clicks and groups. Birds of the same feather type of scenarios. Well, it's true in business it's true in life. I noticed this to be true in sales. Who do you attract to? Well, I made few mistakes. I was and still am a super friendly guy. I will talk to anyone on the sales floor. I would chat with a low producer and the top producer alike. What I realized though, both low producer and the top producer would have influence on my production. For a while I was an average producer. Then I changed my affiliations. and everything changed.

I remember the day I was promoted into the management. The owner of the dealership called me into his office, congratulated me and then told me the following - *"Tony remember you are not part of them any longer (by them he meant the sales people). You are part of us now."* You guessed what he meant by *"us."* It may sound weird or too pretentious right now, but back then I knew what he meant. Yes, I was still on the same team – sales people and managers, but I was not going to be influenced by sales people any longer or by their clicks.

I was a part of a leadership team that was responsible for results produced by the entire team. From that point on a management team was my influence. Well, of course I was still friends with the sales people. I came from their ranks. We were still friends, but my role has changed and with that changed my outlook. No longer I was thinking with *"me"* in the center of all actions and decisions I had to make as a manager, from here on I had to think with *"what's best for the team"* approach. My sphere of influence has changed to a certain degree. Now, my team of managers was influencing me.

In personal life I seek out successful people to be associated with. Both of my friends and bosses are super successful individuals and working with them have changed my life tremendously. I have learned a lot from them. Matured in the business and personal life. But finances are not the only measuring stick of influence. With five children we have had a blessing to be associated with successful parents who were mentors and teachers to us.

In life, if you want to succeed you want to meet people and seek out people from a greater economic status. It only makes sense to learn from someone who have done it before and is willing to share their success tips with you. Sooner or later you will become that person of influence to influence people around you. Then it will be your turn to send an "elevator" down. I have had a privilege to be a mentor to my nephews. One of them is a successful photographer and business owner in Europe, now. Touching lives of people who are willing to learn and eager to absorb your advice is absolutely rewarding. You simply do not know who you will touch and how your fingerprints will influence the blueprint of their lives.

So, who do you associate yourself with? Who are those five people in your life? It's the people you can pick up the phone and talk to. It's someone you can text or email to get an advice. What about your daily influencers? Are they mediocre sales people? Are they "nay" sayers? Whose voice do you listen to? Ask yourself those questions. If you are not with someone who can lift you and positively influence your life, find a different circle of friends. You are in total control!

People are either lifters or downers. The positive ones will uplift you and the negative ones will drag you down. But it goes way deeper than that. There are plenty of positive people who are not successful in life, whether financially or otherwise. What do you want out of life? What is your definition of success? Each one of us must have our own definition of success and strive to reach it. What is it for you?

I hope you have defined it or have a very good idea what it looks and sounds like. With this in mind, think about this - who are the people that display the level of success you desire? Have you identified those influencers in your life? If so, it is important you become close to those people and observe their behavior attentively. To take it a step further, it is not enough to simply observe their behavior, it is important to get to know them by communicating with them and learning from conversations with them. If success breeds success – influence is a big part of this breeding.

I have been fortunate and blessed to associate myself with some very successful people. With English as my second language, being influenced by successful people allows me to acquire the language of success. Having breakfast with a multimillionaire and being able to pick his brain, helps me grow in my understanding of business. Working side by side with an entrepreneur allows me to grow my own risk-taking muscles. Listening to the successful sales person opens my eyes to what is possible in sales world. What do you learn? Better yet, from whom do you learn? Who will you become when you grow up and mature in success? To define all of it you must keep asking yourself questions and take actions based on the answers.

Here are three ways to improve your sphere of influencers.

1. Review all your relationships and rate them on the scale of one to five with the following questions:
   - how positive is their influence on me?
   - is there a drama in their lives that drags me down?
   - does their social-economic status motivate me to excel?
   - am I learning from them to improve my status?

There are plenty more questions to ask, but for now focus on those four. Their positive influence on you matters. Do they have drama in their lives? This matters. Typically, the amount of drama in one's life is a direct reflection of someone's maturity. I have seen people who can never get rid of drama. It follows them all the time. It does not matter where they are in life, where they are in relationships, drama seems to envelop them and be a constant that never change. It is critical to distance yourself from these type of individuals.

2. Ask yourself, *"if I have to make a life changing decision who are my influencers?"* Life changing decisions can be – going to school, moving to another state, getting a new job, investment decision, real estate questions, etc. It is of most importance to bounce ideas and plans from someone you trust and respect. Those influencers in your life are there to guide you and insure you are making a good decision long term. If you are currently do not have anyone in your life who can provide wisdom of making a good decision you are in the world of hurt. Drop everything and begin searching for someone you can add to your circle of relationship. Unless you live on the island and "Wilson" has to be your influencer, you can find someone close by to bring the value of life's wisdom to you.

   This person can be your supervisor, your old teacher or coach, if you are fortunate it can be your family member whom you can trust and who is successful enough to provide you great counsel. My dad does not live nearby; he is about 9000 miles away. Many years ago I made a decision to seek out mentors or influencers in my life. I affiliated myself with several successful business people. Throughout my life I have referred to them with questions. Bouncing ideas and sharing dilemmas was and still is very beneficial. As I progressed I have moved on to add more people who support me in different areas of my life. Adding those people have been extremely helpful. So number two is – seek people who are further than you are in the pursuit of happiness and who can add more value to your life. Make sure it is not a one-way street and offer to provide valuable service back if possible.

3. Speaking of value - seek to add value first. It is easy to get into a cycle of *"me-me-me."* It is not all about you. People around you need to feel and see you are adding value back. When you provide some form of service or give of your time and efforts, it may be not going back directly to those who influence your life. It may be toward someone who is in need of your help. You can be rest assured that it will not go wasted. By giving of yourself to others you will generate much positive influence yourself and it will come back to your ten times fold. I have seen it happen in my life. Positive influence you spread will go around, just like the old saying says – *"what goes is around comes around."* This world has too many negative things happening to all of us and sometimes when you slow down or stop for a moment you can appreciate little positive things that maybe not noticeable. Not sure how I got off the track here. The bottom line, positive influence you share will come back to you in your life.

In sales your mindset is the most important assets you possess. If you are not careful you can easily lose focus and get distracted by negativity of those who may be around you. Your mindset affects your internal fortitude that makes you stronger in sales situations. Your sale can easily evaporate if you are not fully prepared to deliver. This is why those around you either help or hurt your efforts. When negative people or those with lesser aspirations become your sphere of influence you will be affected, whether you want it or not.

Here are the three things you can do to grow in influence

1. Analyze the people in your life – who brings positive who brings negative energy in your life.

2. Seek positive influencers in your world. Surround yourself with as many successful people as you possibly can

3. Be a positive influencer yourself. Spread what you learn and what wisdom you gain.

MY TAKEAWAYS:

I will start _____

_____
_____
_____
_____
_____
_____
_____
_____
_____
_____

I will stop _____

_____
_____
_____
_____
_____
_____
_____
_____
_____
_____
_____

UNDERSTAND HOW TO LOWER SALES RESISTANCE.

CHAPTER 4

Every one of us have a built-in sales resistance. Remember the time you felt being sold? Someone was really pressuring you to reach into your wallet and give them your credit card? Or the time when you were pitched something so bad and you were turned off by their pitch, yet they kept on pushing you? Well, that internal feeling or what I call a BS meter that makes you recognize someone is selling you on something, is part of most of us.

And if you have been exposed to a multitude of pitches you probably much more attuned to it. Well, no one likes to be sold. Being sold feels like someone is taking advantage of you. This negative emotion raises your natural built-in sales resistance – you raise your hand and say STOP! I don't want any of this! Right? We all experienced this. Again you do not like to be sold. Yet, you like to buy. Right? That positive emotion when you willfully pull your wallet and can't wait to buy this – whatever it is. You may so it on the impulse or you may do because you have planned and saved over the weeks, months or even years to purchase this item.

So what is it within us that recognizes the negatives of that pitch and makes us want to run away? Well, at the very core of this is someone's inability to communicate to us what they are pitching in a way that would make us want to reach for our wallet. The difference between top earners in sales and mediocre sales people is their approach and communication ability. As the old saying goes - *"sales are made and lost by few words."* Another sales wisdom says – **it's not what you say it is how you say it.** I would want to add – **It's not what you say, it's how you say it and when you say it.** The sequence of the word track just as important.

But let's go back to what makes us recognize and dislike a bad pitch? Last year several scientists performed a study that pointed out how people react to verbal communication. They were able to detect how a person perceives trustworthiness of an individual by making people listen to one word - "hello." The way a person said this word – the tone, inflection and all of it pointed to person's trustworthiness. One word?!!! This makes things really interesting, right? So what was it in our brain that would make the decision about person intent if you will? Let's take a look at what neuroscientists are saying how our brain process information.

Our brain consists of three parts. At the core is the primitive part – often referred to as a reptilian brain – or lizard brain. This part of the brain is very reactionary. It is where fight or flight resides. In essence it is a gateway to processing all incoming information – a filter in a sense. This filter is responsible for weeding out the unnecessary information or events and passes the urgent or important info to the next part of the brain to deal with it. In other words – it watches out for your survival – be it physical or financial.

The next part of the brain is referred to as the limbic or mid-brain. It is responsible for anything that has to do with emotions, social context and interactions, relational items. This is where trust is established. Some researchers are saying that 90% of all the decisions are based on emotions. This part of the brain controls how we feel about events and information. So this is extremely critical part of our brains – this is the buying part of the brain. What's also important, is to remember it is all about how you make people feel.

Think about it. When you feel good about the situation or a person, it is typically when you had no conflict and there was no friction, right? Oh, you may have been in conflict right before someone made you feel good about things. Something happened. They either said something soothing or did something that pleased you, and you felt good. In most cases when you feel good about something your brain associates that feeling with the person who made you feel that way. Same works in the opposite direction. Your brain quickly recognizes someone who made you feel bad or uneasy and you want to avoid anything that would have to do with this person or deal they represent.

Because of this you want to focus on the emotional part of the deal. When you do this and truly make people feel great about everything – you will get their mid-brain react positively towards you. That includes buying from you.

The third part of our brain is neocortex. It is responsible for numbers and logic. It deals with complex issues in our lives. This is also the area where the buyer's remorse dwells. Right? Did you ever buy something and then later regretted why you spent the money? You were feeling great about the purchase, but later you began counting and then thought, what have I done? We all been there. Again, it is the neocortex that is responsible for all of this.

Ok, you're thinking what does it all have to do with sales? Well, it has everything to do with sales. You see the lizard brain is the gatekeeper. It filters the information and if it finds things unimportant and boring it will shut the brain down and no matter how great the product is you will not buy it. You simply have no interest. So, the path to the mid brain - the emotional aspect of buying decision, is through the primitive brain – the lizard brain. When you bypass the lizard brain you will get through and begin to establish trust with the buyer. Without trust sales transactions rarely happen. To earn trust could take time. The best way to do it is to extend trust to your customer. Sounds easy? Not so fast, lizard.

First and foremost, your pitch has to be – interesting, thought provoking, pattern interrupting, surprising and urgent. The information cannot be boring and old news. It has to be presented from an angle that the buyer would not expect it to be presented from. This will help you bypass the lizard brain and get to the limbic brain.

So, if you sound just like everybody else, you will be passed. When you begin getting through you begin creating what I call – buyer curiosity. When the buyer becomes curios about you and your offering, sale resistance begins to evaporate slowly. Now this is very fragile situation. The buyer can lose the curiosity very quickly. You have to handle it with care and keep feeding this curiosity. This is where your pitch critical. You want to win? You have to work on your pitch. I will cover your pitch later in another chapter. Once you create a message that is all of the above you can begin connecting with the midbrain.

This is very powerful. You must never use it for evil - Ha! Yes, being able to influence someone to make a decision is an interesting and powerful thing. When this person arrives at their own decision to make a decision that is when you know you have arrived. There is more than one way to lower sales resistance.

Persuading someone to a decision is an art. What I like about this art is anyone can learn how. I do want to mention that manipulation is an enemy of a salesperson. Persuading and manipulation are two different things. No one likes to be manipulated into making a decision especially when they are spending money. On the other hand, when someone helped you arrive at your own decision to reach into your wallet and spend your money, it's different. You feel better when you were the one that made this decision and it was your idea and not someone else's. It is as if the sales person was really a facilitator of your decision, a guide, a coach who helped you make a buying decision.

Remember the midbrain is the social, emotional and relational. You heard this saying - *people like to buy from someone they like and trust?* Well, this is why. The midbrain is where it all happens. But people don't like you or trust you when they first meet you. You have to work on that. Then there is a Neocortex. The part of the brain that is responsible for logic, numbers and reason. You want to stay off numbers until you have the mid brain engaged. Ok. How do you get through this lizard brain and lower sales resistance?

Step ONE: you must understand how it works.

It is a built-in self-preservation mechanism that all of us poses and utilize often when we are exposed to new situations involving sales people. Look once you understand that and know that it is natural for people to protest a sales pitch, then you know it is not personal and it is universal reaction. Well, now you know, what else?

Likeability happens fast – one word, one move, tone and inflection. Everything about your communication. Will they like the way you look, smell, walk and talk? You decide. Why create extra work for yourself? Why create extra objections?

Most of the time sales people create their objections with the way they walk, talk, look and smell. Think about it. What makes you like the sales or service person from the first few minutes of communication with an individual? First impressions if you will? Did they smile? Do you perceive them as approachable? Do they have a pep in their walk? Do they communicate with the right amount of urgency? Are they eager to help you? Do their body language communicate "I'm here to serve you?" Do they listen? How many times you met someone who interrupted you and wanted to push their agenda? Does this lowers sales resistance or raise it? I covered what we all experience, so now you must work on reverse engineering this thing.

Step Two: Be likeable.

Look when you reverse engineer the bad experience = what would turn you off when you deal with people you arrive at what is needed to lower sales resistance. Being likeable will lower the sales resistance barrier. Being likeable may sounds easy but it is not. I have seen many nice people stiff up when they are dealing with people.

I mean they are great when they are not under pressure but the moment they are in sales situation they feel pressure and become more mechanical filled with word tracks and scripts. The best advice I could give you is BE yourself – relax. Be real – people like real people. If you are trying to be someone that you are not, they will see right through you. Top sales people are relaxed and intense at the same time. Smile, firm handshake, look them in the eyes. When you focus on helping them and not yourself you will act different. Start liking them. When you like first they will like you back.

Step Three: Stop selling.

Yes, stop selling. I know this does not make sense. It is counterintuitive. But this is what true professionals are doing. ***They are not selling they are connecting.*** The old adage – ABC – Always Be Closing is DEAD! Your customers are not idiots, they figured it out. Instead best sales people are using new versions of ABCs – Always Be Connecting and Always Be Compelling. When you stop selling and begin connecting instead, people see your true motives. If you are truly care about helping people to get what they want, you will connect with them faster and their sales resistance will disappear.

I received a phone call from one sales person in car business. He said he struggled with his production and was not sure what happened. After listening to him I suggested he stopped trying to sell and instead begin solving his customers' problems. They come to the dealership with a puzzle pieces and his job is to help them put those together. He listened and later that day I got a text from him thanking me – I stopped selling and solved problems for two customers and they bought from him – he helped two people buy vehicles that day – and sold two cars.

Let's review. There are three parts of the brain that work together processing information. The base – croc brain is very primitive it acts as a filter or a gatekeeper for all information in is responsible for your survival be it physical or financial. The mid-brain is where most the decisions are made – it's a trust generator it controls that emotional gut feel – it feels just right type of thing. And then finally the neocortex – it figures numbers calculates risk and sends ok or not ok to the midbrain. The key to lower the sales resistance is to get through the croc brain first. It is about creating trust and likeability with a person.

Here is a recap on how to lower sales resistance:

1. Understand Sales resistance and how it works

2. Be likeable when they like you, you will connect with them faster

3. Stop selling – ABC is dead the new ABC is Always Be Connecting.

MY TAKEAWAYS:

I will start _____

_____
_____
_____
_____
_____
_____
_____
_____
_____
_____

I will stop _____

_____
_____
_____
_____
_____
_____
_____
_____
_____
_____

STRENGTHEN YOUR SALES MUSCLES.

CHAPTER 5

Don Beebe was one of the fastest wide receivers in the NFL. In 1989 during a combine, he ran an impressive 4.21 40-yards dash time. That year at the age of 25 he was drafted by Buffalo Bills. During his NFL career he had six Super Bowl appearances. His impressive career landed him five Championship rings and one Super Bowl ring. He was not the tallest or the strongest but he was one of the fastest. Don went on to work with young kids and built a business – the "House of Speed" where he teaches young athletes how to increase their speed. Don uses three elements to help build muscles that help individuals win in their game by becoming faster. These three things of muscle training are – *Strength, Flexibility and Explosive power.*

When you think of *Strength,* think of your ability to close a deal. This one is always measured by your results. How good are your closing skills? Do you have enough words in your head to create buyer's curiosity and overcome some objections? Every time I make a call to a potential client, I usually play out the conversation in my head before I dial the number. Through some networking I got a hold of a dealer group owner.

Our company have tried to get their business few years ago and failed. Their current provider is very much entrenched and I knew the conversation would have to be short and interesting enough to grab his attention. I focused on the training aspect of our offering. This time it was no different I played through the conversation in my head. My goal was to get on his calendar and secure the meeting.

I dialed the number, cleared my voice and waited for the response. He picked up the phone. I had to speak fast –

"Hi, Nick! This is Tony calling. You do not know me, but you do know the company I represent. I would like to get on your calendar to share with you some cool developments in the training area we have done. When can we meet?"

"Well, I know you guys. And I'm not looking to switch what I'm doing now."

"Nick, I'm not asking you to switch, I want to meet to share with you about the training program that our dealer partners take advantage of."

"Well, we already do training and I would not want to interrupt anything we do. But, stay in touch and get back with me in six months. Thanks!"

"Ok, thank you Nick. I will be in touch."

That was all. I blew it. I got nowhere with him. The standard **"call me in six months or next year"** response was ok, but I knew I blew it. Nick got a tad interested, but it did not translate into an appointment. You see, I knew how to deal with his response - "I'm not interested in switching", my response was "I'm not asking you to switch." Where I failed is I did not anticipate him saying "we got training covered." I was simply not prepared for that one. This is why building your sales muscle is so crucial. You practice and develop your closing muscle during practice.

Preparation allows you to work on possible objections. What if they respond with this? You ask yourself. That is why in practice you work on those scenarios. How strong you are will be determined in the real life situations. You rarely get second chance or a re-do in of the conversation. Coming back with solutions second time around can be perceived weak, too pushy and unprofessional. Get your words right the first time.

Later analyzing my conversation, I realized I could have responded with - *"Of course you have training. I wouldn't expect you not to. Almost all of our clients have some form of training, this is why we need to meet to share with you how our program will fill in the gaps of your current training plan."*

Now, in hindsight it's always 20/20, right? I do not know if Nick would have flopped for an appointment or not. One thing I do know; is this it might have given me more chances. In Russian we have a saying **"the spoon is better during lunch."** It means a solution is better at the time you need it and not after the fact. This was the very first time I faced this type of objection, and I did not anticipate it to come up in the conversation. The lesson is, even with the best preparation you can never know what objections will be thrown at you. This does not mean you should not be preparing. I'd rather over prepare and stumble deep in the conversation, vs. no preparation and get washed away with a first "no."

Being Flexible during sales process is opposite of being rigid. Thanks Captain Obvious! On a serious note, one of the most powerful human desires is the desire to be right. In addition to that, most sales people possess a very competitive spirit. This is great, but if not used properly, it can lead you to be more rigid and less flexible. This can be dangerous during negotiating situations. Winning is everything, and being flexible can lead you to more wins than you think. When you let them win it will pay dividends in a long run.

When it comes to *Explosive Power* think in terms how it starts so it goes. False starts will cause your sale to sputter and stall. To achieve maxim results you have to move fast and be swift in your approach. Waiting for things to happen, usually don't provide you explosive growth opportunities.

Over the years I became friends with Coach Jay Wolf of Starshooter.net. Jay spent his lifetime training and coaching young athletes on how to shoot and score in the game of basketball. After attending his workshop sessions, they improve their shooting capabilities by a high margin. Jay worked with NCAA schools and NBA teams. He is a passionate student of the game. His system is simple and involves three steps – *Vertical Alignment, One Hand Release and Arc Power.* He teaches kids that success is all about details and that nothing comes easy. The importance of practice and self-diagnostics are most important to improve one's skills. Talking to kids, Jay speaks of being your own "doctor" to diagnose problems they have with their vertical alignment, one hand release or arc power. *"Are you a sloppy doctor or a fussy one?"* he asks them. Self-diagnostics require focus and focus is hard to come by for most sales people. It is easy to get distracted and lose it. This requires sales maturity which does not come easy.

Practice also allows one to get things close to perfection in the controlled environment. In Jay's words – **"Perfection is learned on the free-throw line and not in the game - the speed of the game kills perfection"** and **"there is no do-overs in the game of basketball."** Think how true this is in sales! The sale can evaporate in seconds and you have no chance of recovery. Your client rebuffs your statement and you have no comeback, just like my conversation with Nick.

Your tools are your words. How good are you with your words? How good are you with your presentation? Did you master your pitch and know your customer's most common objections? Can you score when the speed of the game increases? Can you keep-up with the speed of the game? It is obvious why both Don Beebe and Jay Wolf advocate repetition of movements their students must master in order to perform during the game at the highest level possible.

How often do you practice? How often do you reflect on your performance? Do you "watch the tape?" Do you analyze your actions? When it comes to diagnosing your performance flaws, are you a sloppy or fussy doctor? You cannot strengthen the muscles you need during the game if you are practicing wrong, if you are not focused and not paying attention to correcting your game. To recap, here are five things you can do to improve your chances, and me more prepared for your sales encounters:

1. Develop a practicing system that works for you

2. Practice your pitch to perfection in the controlled environment

3. Always review your practice performance

4. Be a fussy doctor and do a self-diagnostic to improve skills

5. Repetition is the key – practice, practice, practice

MY TAKEAWAYS:

I will start _____
_____
_____
_____
_____
_____
_____
_____
_____
_____

I will stop _____
_____
_____
_____
_____
_____
_____
_____
_____
_____
_____

BE A HUNTER AND KNOW HOW TO RUN CIRCLES AROUND YOUR COMPETITION.

CHAPTER 6

Sales jobs involve either getting new business – *hunting* or keeping and growing existing business – *farming*. In this chapter you will learn few ideas on how to out-sell your competition. If you are a hunter and gatherer this one is for you. If you are a farmer – responsible for growth and development of existing business you will learn about it in the next chapter. I have done and currently I'm doing both hunt/gather and farm as well, and I love to run circles around my competition.

The great thing about free market, is the fact that there are plenty of choices for customers and businesses. It is the best thing ever! It also means you will have plenty of the competition to deal with. When it comes to how to deal with it, there are two extremes – **ignore it or worry too much about it.**

So you can burry your head into the ground and pretend it does not exist, then one day you will wake up to a different reality and realize that it is too late to change things. Your competition took your business away or they outsold you on the proposal and got the deal. The other extreme is – you worry about competition all the time. You operate as if they are out to kill your deal and undercut you or get your existing business. You may call me crazy, but this crazy Russian wants to live in this reality. They are out there to get my business. I'm paranoid as if they are KGB who listen to my phone conversations. Maybe not *that* crazy. The bottom line I love my competition and hate it at the same time. It forces me to be better. It forces me to practice and hone my skills, it forces me to be strategic, it forces me to close deals, it forces me to keep business.

Here is the thing you want to reach the level where you are paranoid and confident at the same time you must be there! It's when inside you know you run circles around them, but you also know that at any moment they could creep up and get your business. I found that keeping this balance is super important.

I have been in sales since 14 years old. Back on the wild streets of Leningrad USSR. At the time my competition was protected by Russian mafia. This is why it was risky business to be in. The other side of that coin was the law enforcement. During Soviet days police in the USSR was extremely corrupted, actually that probably did not change much. Well, they were on the other side of mafia trying to compete with them for control of space. I had to walk a narrow road in order to stay away from both. It was kind of a school of hard knocks – really it was. There were couple of cases where I got physically threatened, but I was lucky and got out of the situations unscathed. So how do you run circles around your competition?

Number One – Be credible.

Be credible. Business people absolutely get it. They see right through you if you are not credible. This has to show in your walk, talk and actions. It takes so long to build it and you can lose credibility with just one bad move. Look, I made plenty of mistakes during my life. I remember one really bad one. I was in pitching mode and got carried away with one feature of the program, that I was not super familiar with and made a claim, which was true but when the person asked me a question I dug deeper into the unknown and dug a deeper hole for myself. I made statement regarding tax advantage of this part of the program, what I did not realized or knew the person I was talking to in his past life was a tax CPA and he called me out on my statement. Again the statement was true, but I could not back it up. I lost credibility within seconds. The meeting was over, right there and then. I screwed up, my attempts to fix it later with addressing his concerns were fruitless. I messed up an opportunity, all because I spoke about something I was not knowledgeable about.

Number Two – Become an expert.

Ok, being an expert helps your credibility. An expert is someone who is knowledgeable in a particular industry and its intricate parts. This specialized knowledge is what makes you an expert. You can speak of it not just in general terms but in specific terms it's because you actually practiced it and lived it, not just read it on the internet while googling it.

Studying any subject does not make you an expert, it is both studies and applied knowledge that elevates your status. People respect someone who lives what they are talking about. I tell you I met so many decision makers and it is a game changer for me when I can speak their language and understand their world, it is only because I lived it. Keep working on your skills, know your product or services in and out. Read more than anyone else. Buy books, audiobooks, magazines, and online publications and most importantly don't dig holes you cannot get out of, like in my story with a tax guy.

Number Three – Get to the decision maker.

Stop wasting time with pitching your ideas or trying to get meeting with the people who cannot make a decision! Yea, yea I know sometimes you got to win friends and have allies. Bull crap. You don't need allies. People will rarely carry water for you. You need the decision maker who can tell you yes or no. So how do you effectively get in front of one? Look there are no easy answers or a magic pill out there that would help you grow a pair of gorilla balls.

Most people are afraid of bosses whether they are theirs or someone else's. Here is a thing if you are afraid of getting in front of the decision maker, because they are a boss, you will rarely get in front of them. You must stop thinking in hierarchy terms, the proverbial **"bow down and kiss the ring"** will not get you there.

When you start thinking about a decision maker as a regular person a guy or a gal just like you, call them by their first name – not Mr… Or Mrs… It's *"hi John, Hi Tammy."* So first of all, get over your fears. Second of all get on their calendar, get a meeting. Even if it is only for six minutes. You must be in front of them to get anywhere. Do your research, find out if there are any acquaintances you have who knows them. Be creative, bypass gate keepers and layers of corporate jungles, committees and so forth - get in front of the "big cheese" so you can look at his or hers eyes and do your pitch. Same can be done over the phone. Go ahead, when you make your next phone call, just ask him or her by their first name. Act as if you are an old friend, you'll bypass most gate keepers.

Number Four – Perfect your Pitch.

If there is one thing you take away is this – *you must perfect your pitch.* If you are winging it every time you are not going to win.

First get the order of your pitch down, come up with a killer opening and a killer call to action – close. Make sure the middle is all meat. Keep it short. People don't have much attention span nowadays. Keeping your pitch short will allow you to keep their attention and will get you more business.

Finally keep it simple. If it is overly complicated you will get ignored, if you are all numbers you will get ignored, if you are too slow and boring, you will get ignored. You want to generate questions and engage your audience. I have been involved in thousands of pitching situations from pitching both in business to consumer and business to business. You have to keep in conversational and not sales-y. I hear sales people pitch me their ideas and products and more often than not, I'm getting blown away how they are either don't get prepared or pitch things so horribly that it turns me off right away.

When you grab my attention with a great opening and then keep me engaged throughout the presentation, by stimulating my imagination you, then you close with a compelling message – call to action – all the while keeping it short you will win most of the time!

Here are some problems with most sales people's pitch – they try too hard- pushing their agenda, they sound smarmy, they are too long, they fumble around, there is little to know structure to their pitch, they are inconsistent in their delivery, they are consistent with being lame, they are not prepared, they have killer close, they are arrogant, they use too many slides, they don't know their material, they are reading data or use too much data, they cannot frame their message, they have no message, they use we language.

What most don't realize is, this "we" language is huge mistake. *"We can do this we help get this, we…we…we…we…we."* People are sick of it. Look, turn your pitch into a winning pitch with **YOUR** language. When *you* partner with us here is what *you* get…. Another way to frame it is by using your existing clients' stories – Not what we are doing for our clients, but rather here are the results our clients getting by utilizing this approach. There are couple of great books out there – *Pitch Anything and The Art of a Pitch*. Both are short reads and very well in describing how to win presentations with your perfected pitch. To perfect your pitch – write it out, practice it, use it, re-write it, practice some more and then use it again. It is a never ending process. You will know when you nailed it though – they will say yes more often.

My closing ratio has gone up sky high when I perfected my pitch. One time I was pitching our company to a dealer group and I started with a strong framing statement – *"Look guys, after this presentation 80% of dealers decide to do business with us"*, this is a true statement, I pause for effect and let it sink in. *"The other 20 percent think we are full of crap"* I say with a smile. One guy said so your closing ratio is 80% - yes captain obvious! You might have several pitches. Some really short, while others are presentations length. Whatever it is keep tweaking it and tweaking it until it's perfect. I have a pitch for setting a meeting, a pitch to present my company and then ask for a business analysis, then another pitch for presentation of our findings. Every single one of those has been defined and re-defined. All right I will share more about pitch later.

Number Five – Close like a crazy Russian.

Close the deal! Here is what I find many sales people do, they prepare, they present and then fail to ask for business, they just let customer walk out or they walk out after presentation without the next step. After your presentation, the next step should be either – please sign here or here is the follow up plan. Some transactions are taking time to close, I get it. What I mean is many sales people weren't prepared to ask for a deal. They simply fizzled out. They were as weak as a circus lemonade at the end. I love that phrase. Actually never tried circus lemonade but I'm sure it's weak.

Look you MUST close the deal! You MUST ask for a sale! You MUST get over your fear of a "no" and get their commitment! In simple terms and in most cases deals are either closed on the spot, delayed decision, or rejected. There really no other outcomes. By the way before you pitch your presentation establish the fact that you will ask them for business at the end. That way there are no surprises. When you lay out your game plan at the beginning your will prepare them for close, also you might get some objections early enough and could handle them throughout your presentation.

People ask me how do I ask for business? I mean there are so many different ways to do it. Ideally you guide your customer with your presentation so it arrives at a natural conclusion of them saying what do I need to do next? That really is the best way is when they arrive at the conclusion and close themselves. Now I'm a realist it does not happen often all the stars have to align. With that said you must help align the stars. The biggest star of this whole thing has to be them. You make them feel like a star and help them make this decision. In other cases, you simply tell them what the next step is and give them the choice when they want to get started. If your presentation is a conversation, then the close is conversational as well. You can speak of pros and cons out loud as if you are them. Help them sort things out and then simply ask for the order. Here is the reality, the longer you wait the harder they are to come to a decision. So you got to move quickly. Urgency is of a foremost importance. This is why the next step is critical!

Number Six – Follow-up, follow-up and more follow-up!

This is another area that most sales people miss. They don't establish the next step and then don't know when and how to follow-up or worse yet, don't follow-up at all. It's amazing. Several years ago I had three companies come and give me a quote to replace the roof on my house. The fact that the quotes were several thousand apart was not a big deal, I get it.

I really liked one guy who gave me a quote, because he was very personable. His numbers were in the middle of the other two guys. I told him to let me get couple of things in order and that he should check with me in a couple of weeks. I'm still waiting for his call. I mean they must have been busy to skip on a $10,000 job. I simply don't get it.

Here is the deal, when you establish the next step the follow-up is much easier to do. They know why you are calling or visiting. Without the next step follow-up is awkward. Let's say they tell you they will be making a final decision next month after they have two more presentations (oops I hope you knew that prior the presentation),

"Great then the next is I will be calling you guys on the XX date of the month to see how it went. Let me check the calendar, hm would Tuesday the week of the 3rd work for you? Good, morning or afternoon? Great I'll call you that morning at 9:15."

You are set. Now it does not mean you are not to get them some additional info sometime in between or swing by the place if you are in the area.

"Hey, I know we are on in couple of weeks, I was just in the area and wanted to see how your meetings are going?"

Cool? Now, be in touch! If you feel this is doable go for it. It all depends how your relationships were with those folks. Here are couple of tips –

- Number one identify who you are will be following up with,
- Number two make sure you get their cell number, if you don't have it yet.

Now you can text if you have not done it before. I closed a $250,000 annual profit deal via text – it was after three months of follow up. Now this is a three year relationships! Which leads me to the final part.

The only thing is, you MUST follow-up! Do not miss opportunities. Do not be a dummy, like my roofing guy(s).

Number seven – Never give-up and take a NO for an answer.

Most sales people give up too soon. They try to knock on the door few times and when they get nowhere they back up and walk away. This is why if you hang on there you will be the last man standing. You will run circles around your competition.

Statistically most sale people give up way too soon to get to the decision maker. If they do get to one they don't close and or don't follow-up and get the deal to conclusion. I had few deals that took me six months to close, now these are large ticket residual income deals.

But the longest period of persistence I have seen is one of my co-workers – Heidi. She has been told no from one business owner several times, but she kept being in front of him and got the deal – it took her four years! She closed it after four years!!! Really??? Way to go to hang in there. I mean everyone on the team told her she should just move on and leave those guys. She kept getting new business but never gave up on this client. At the end she wore them out with her persistence and won! Persistence wares out the resistance. When you get a no – ask why? When you keep getting a no – figure out how to get to a yes. Sometimes it is when you walk away from the deal and step aside you can see an answer through a different angle. Never GIVE UP! Never, ever give up!

Ok, here you go! Are you ready to run circles around your competition? If you are not out there to get their lunch money they will get yours! Get your share of the business and win! Win in every area of your process. Be better than they are at everything. Don't stick your head into the sand and ignore your competition.

These seven things helped me and my team. There are plenty of other things you can do to outsell your competition. But here my seven:

1. Be credible – it the starting point

2. Be an expert in your field – when you a pro it shows

3. Get in front of the decision maker – he or she holds the keys

4. Perfect your pitch! - you must master your presentations

5. Close like crazy! - you must ask for the deal several times

6. Follow-up times 100! - establish the next step and get busy

7. Never give up and take a no for an answer – be the last person standing

MY TAKEAWAYS:

I will start _____

_____
_____
_____
_____
_____
_____
_____
_____
_____
_____

I will stop _____

_____
_____
_____
_____
_____
_____
_____
_____
_____
_____
_____

BE A FARMER AND KNOW HOW TO RUN CIRCLES AROUND YOUR COMPETITION.

CHAPTER 7

In the last chapter you learned about how you can win if you are a hunter in sales. You go out there and get new business for your company or yourself. If you are in car sales for instance or in real estate sales, you out there hunting for new biz every day, right? So now you got the business what do you do to keep it and how do handle your existing customers? Listen I ran into so many sales people who are great hunters and do nothing about their existing customer base. Remember I came out of car biz and car guys are known to be very transaction-oriented. You sold a car and don't care what happens next, right? When did you heard from your car sales person after he got your business? If you are lucky, you get a true professional and he or she will stay in touch and it won't be *"hey, send me some referrals."* If you are not in transactional business (Best Buy) where relationships truly matter you stay with your clients and service their needs.

As I stated before I have done both business to customer and business to business sales. In business to business is important to have an aggressive or defensive minded approach. You want to keep the competition away and preferably have relationships with your new client/partner for years to come. I can tell you that this is not as easy as it sounds.

SO here are seven things you can do to keep the competition away and run circles around them.

Number One – Be an expert!

YES. It sounds very similar to the previous chapter, but different. When you are an expert you are wanted by both prospective clients and your existing clients as well. An expert will advise his current clients on whatever their needs are in his field of knowledge. One advice or one recommended idea could save your clients thousands of dollars and this is hard to replace.

When you are building new business relationship you are also tested from time to time, especially early on. This is why an expert status is so desirable. If they cannot find an answer with you believe me they will find it with someone else, typically your competition. You will find out later when you have been replaced. Being an expert also allows you to drive great results to your clients as well as getting the most out of this relationship. Ask yourself *"do I have 100% of my client's valet or do I share it with my competition?"* When you are an expert you gain trust and respect, this allows you to get your products and services into all areas where your client can use them.

Bottom line, you must work towards getting an expert status with your current clients. Again, an expert is someone with an extensive knowledge and or experience in a particular field. BE THAT PERSON! Do more than you are expected to do for your clients. Learn more about your job, so you can become indispensable to them. Positioning yourself as an expert will help you become a true partner and trusted advisor for them. That is what you are striving to be. When your client has an issue that may not be in line of services you provide, find a solution for them. When you bring it to them, it will go a long way, even though it may not benefit you right away. Over time, you will build up the status of a reliable, trusted advisor and that's my friend will pay you dividends BIG time! More on this later. Know this, when they come to you and ask you for more, everyone will win! That is how you get more of their wallet.

Number Two – Treat your business as if someone is trying to steal it from you.

Mark Cuban the owner of Dallas Mavericks once said *"Work like there is someone working 24 hours a day to take it away from you."*

As I mentioned before there are two extremes to look at the competition – one is burry your head into sand and pretend it does not exist and act like that. The last one is too expensive. But many businesses choose to operate this way. The one I prefer is being borderline paranoid about someone taking business away from me. I'd rather take the billionaire's take on it. I choose to work so hard **because** there is someone who will take it away from me, if I'm careless.

Now I get it, sometimes there just nothing you can do about someone else coming in and swooping your business away from you, but there are ways to keep it. The author of "Good to Great", Jim Collins, wrote another book called "How Mighty Fall." In that book he illustrates how certain companies over the years of economic ups and downs avoided falling hard. While other companies failed miserably, these companies thrived.

One underlining thing about those companies that was different from the companies that fell hard, was the fact that they did not relax. They achieved great success, but instead of plato-ing and then falling hard, they caught themselves prior to plato-ing and forced another rise. When you are not taking things for granted and focus on keeping business with intensity your will operate on a different level. This also shows in your attitude and behavior when you visit with your clients.

You have outwork and outperform the competition. You must deliver such results that your clients will turn the competition away, when it shows up on their front door. This is why this next one is critical

Number Three- Be a partner not a vendor.

Let me be straight with you - having a vendor status sucks. Sorry, actually, I'm not. What happens when you visit your client, do people avoid you and hide from you? That is what happening to vendors. *"Here he comes again, I better pretend to be busy and stare at my laptop."* Vendors are transactional. I mean if you don't mind transactional business and fine with losing business to competition it's probably fine. I should rephrase it when you are vendor or supplier it is not bad; it is bad if you are perceived as a vendor or a supplier. You are not ranked as high on the relationship's level with your client.

Vendors get re-scheduled and pushed off the calendar, partners most of the time don't need a scheduled meeting or a calendar. By definition partners are in this thing together. If you are in service or consulting business you must achieve this status – become a partner. This is easier said than done, but it is your ultimate goal. I have witnessed my friend become so in-meshed with one company that all employees for a very long time thought he was on the company's payroll, yet he was a consultant. Everything associated with the area of his expertise was going through him, he even became part of the Senior Management team. Now that's positioning!

Partnership is achievable. I have a privilege of being considered a partner-type with several businesses I work with. The owners text me and call me with questions. I feel privileged to have those relationships. Listen, in business relationships are beyond super important. They are YOUR LIFEBLOOD!

Obviously, you must bring value. It rarely happens simply because you share the same interests with your clients – although it helps if you golf, hunt or fish together. But value must be beyond ordinary. Everyone can pull ordinary. It is when you become an extraordinary asset for your client is when you are considered a true partner. Giving of your knowledge, time, care, is the cement that solidifies this foundation. Trust is one major component that goes in this as well.

I used to tell my boys – they are 25, 22 and 18 right now, that we all make deposits into emotional banks of each other every single day. WE can then, in time of needs call upon this emotional bank and withdraw an amount we need. If the account is too low, you need to fill it back up. It is true in relationships within family or friends, it is true in relationships with business partners.

In some cases, there are actual accounts involved. You must put in a lot of emotional deposits to establish and maintain trust. Partners trust each other and that is the foundation for your success with this client. You can count on those deposits when the competition is snooping around. BY the same token if you stop depositing then your account is in the negative and only could last so long. It takes a lot to build true trust-based relationships, yet it takes just one stupid thing to lose it all. Beware. Make sure your intentions and your heart is in the right place.

Maintain relationships. Now it is great to have this type of relationships with the decision maker or makers but what about the rest of the team?

Number Four – Make your business sticky.

Making your business sticky means you are bringing more value than anyone else out there. Remember, their perception is your reality. If your client does not perceive the amount of value, you bring is high enough – it is not high enough. You can be out there busting your back and get no recognition for your efforts, because you did not position yourself the right way. Maybe only one level of managers knows what you are doing and bringing in, but the corporate office has no idea and when asked their opinion about you and your work, they shrug shoulders.

You must figure out how to get credit when it is due. I'm not talking about walking around and saying – *did you see what I did?* Look how great I'm. This is crazy, not Russian-crazy, but simply dumb. This will position you being self-centered and arrogant. This my friend, people do despise.

Ok, how do you do it? First of all, *you must bring massive amounts of value.* When you do that it is value to their organization. It could be something not related to your project or your products. I once brought a lender to help a business with inventory financing and commercial real estate. Switching to this lender helped business save over $100k a year versus their current provider. Now, there was no financial benefit to me directly, but there was a benefit – business owner acknowledged that fact and to this day thank me for helping him arrange the meeting. The direct financial benefit – is this business is still our partner. What can you do to bring them value in other areas of their business?

Take a moment and look at their challenges and figure out a creative way to assist them. It does not need to be extravagant. Part of making your relationship sticky is developing relationships with everyone in the business if possible – pay attention to key people that are influencers. As always, treat everyone with respect when you communicate or visit with them. When you genuinely care about people and show it goes a very long way.

Number Five – Help them drive great results.

If you are in consulting/training services or offer products to your clients it is important that your help them get the most out of what you bring to them. Helping them drive excellent results must be your mission. This ties in with the above points that makes you sticky and in-mashed into their world. In my business my client's results drive everybody's profitability – theirs and ours. Driving great results will also drive the competition away. This does take planning, discipline and consistent execution. Train and coach everyone involved. Be part of forecasting and monitoring progress. When problems arise work through them. Take ownership as you face challenges.

Number Six – Anticipate problems.

Speaking of problems and challenges, you must anticipate them. You cannot place your head into the sand and pretend there are no problems. Things rarely go as smooth as you envision them to go. Because you deal with people, things can become messy. It is nothing bad, it is simply the reality of business relationships. In addition, you might be dealing with technology or third party suppliers who might be shipping something or setting things up. Being proactive with anything you are implementing is super important.

Double and triple check things before you roll them out. Assume things will go wrong and be super sensitive anticipating problems and fixing them proactively. The "Murphy's Law" can be a tough, mitigating side-effects of problems can be much easier if you are not blind-sided by them. Be prepared.

Number Seven – Don't hide from problems.

Face problems head on. If you find out there are issues:
- Number one don't blow them away
- Number two – take ownership
- Number three - be proactive to fix it right away
- Number four - communication. Act fast and be proactive
- Number five- no blame games!

If you begin to point fingers thinking you will distract things and it will go away, you will create separation and that trust we spoke about will be gone. You cannot afford it. Pick up that phone, drive up do whatever it takes to get it taken care of and then abundant communication. Someone once said – ***you own the problem you own the customer.***

Here are the seven things that will help you run circles around your competition:

1. Be an expert – you are a resource to your client
2. Treat your biz as if someone wants to take it away from your
3. Be a partner – relationships are everything
4. Make your business sticky – add massive value
5. Help them drive great results – continue with support
6. Anticipate problems – they will happen
7. Face problems head on – own the problem own the customer's

No matter if you are a hunter or a farmer or both, to succeed you must operate on a different level than your competition. It takes extra hard work to be a super star in sales. Sales can be a bloody sport. ***It takes a lot to be number one*** – this was what my old boss used to say. Whenever he said this I knew what he meant – he was challenging my commitment's level. I always took it in a positive way because I wanted to win. Hey I want you to win. Your family want you to win. Do you want to win? Winning is not easy, because if it was easy everyone would do it. Right? And, in the words of a legendary coach Vince Lombardi – *"winning is everything."*

MY TAKEAWAYS:

I will start _____

I will stop _____

SEVEN AND A HALF WAYS TO POSITION YOURSELF FOR A PROMOTION.

CHAPTER 8

A while ago, my friend Paul Walser, a big time car dealer, said that *"The best opportunities are the ones that come to you."*

Over the years I thought about this and looking back I realized that this is very true in my life. I had so many opportunities come my way in some cases bigger than I ever expected. I mean I'm an immigrant from Russia, English is my second language. Yet, I had an opportunity to be a General Manager of a top 100 Toyota dealerships in the United States. Twice I had a privilege to speak at National Automotive Dealer Association Convention – it is like a speaker's Olympics for automotive speakers.

Twice I was one of ten International judges for Hyundai's First Global Sales Consultant Championship in Seoul, Korea. I trained managers in the Middle East and spoke at the conference in Portugal. I write articles that are published both online and in print. Not too shabby for a Russian immigrant who had a "C" in English at school. Well, all those opportunities came to me. I started as a sales person at a car dealership back in 1997. It took few years to get to where I am now. Over the 14 years in the car dealership, I was a sales person, finance manager, new car manager, finance director, used car manager, corporate finance director, corporate director of training, and a general manager. Out of those eight positions, I only asked for two. The other ones were presented to me.

Now, I can make a claim here, the opportunities which come to you when you are not begging for them or running around to generate them, are better for you. This is because people come to you and when you are the prize things are looking really good! You always want to position yourself as a prize. When that happens, you get paid better because you have more leverage. You want more leverage and you want better paying opportunities, right?

So, the question is, how do you position yourself in such a way that opportunities do come to you? This does not mean you sit around and wait for things to happen, instead you keep positioning yourself and repositioning yourself to the point you are wanted. I'll share with seven ways that worked for me. Here is what my experience has been, there is never a single thing that makes a difference, and it is always a combination of several things. So here is my list:

Number one – show up early.

Hey, this seems like a small thing but your current employer and your future one do care about this. By the way, in business when you show up early your client will see that and appreciate it as well.

I'm utterly amazed how many people seem to miss this one. Look you do not have to be a rocket scientist to get up on time and show up to work early. If you struggle with this now, when you work a 9 to 5 sales gig, now imagine getting up at 3am to catch a 5am plane for a business meeting in another state? (By the way, sometimes businesses that offer those opportunities will be much more lucrative ones.) So if your shift starts at 9, gets there at 8 or 8:30. First of all, your boss might be already there and while you are getting ready for your day, you might find a customer or two. It happened to me many of times.

You are building your future now. Every missed work day, every time you are late to work you are building an impression of who you are. It also becomes a part of your fiber or character. Being punctual and early pays. Now, everyone can have a second chance. But why mess up now when you can build your future right now. Start with a great work ethic. Treat your current job as if it was the best job ever. When you show up early you show up on time and in addition to building a habit - you are positioning yourself for a great future.

Number two - be prepared.

This may sound simple, but when you show up on time, make sure you are ready. This is why when you are early by 30 -45 mins you have plenty of time to prepare yourself for your day. It gives you time to gather your thoughts, plan out your day, make some early calls or send those emails to follow up clients.

Planning your day, week, month and year takes time and when you have planned things you are prepared to face your day, week, month and year. Ask yourself, *what skills do you need to work on? Is it phone skills, presentation skills, closing skills??* Whatever they are you must be prepared.

Being early also gives you an opportunity to practice, drill and rehearse your pitch. Always prepare yourself for customer experience. Practice your presentation. Be prepared for possible objections and think about eliminating them all together. On top of being prepared for your customer, be prepared for your boss. Know and understand what style of leadership your boss operates in. How much information does she needs from you? How detailed does it needs to be? Navigating corporate world can be difficult, but once you figure it out it will be much easier for your to be prepared for meetings with your boss.

Being prepared also means you are preparing yourself for your next stage – be it promotion into management or senior associate. So be prepared, you never know when your boss or a headhunter calls on you with an opportunity.

Number three – set goals.

This might be an overdone or over-advised thing. Most likely you heard about goals one million times. Right? Well, it's part of the deal. Get yourself into goal setting, forecasting and tracking mindset. I used to set personal goals, then departmental goals, later my team and I set goals for an entire dealership with 135 employees. Now I help businesses set and reach goals. No matter what position you are in it is never too late to start setting goals, forecasting and tracking your progress. Make sure you set your sights high. There is no reason to chase small or mediocre goals.

Number four – never complain.

This might seem like an easy thing to do. Except, most people are complainers. They complain about anything and everything that does not goes their way. Some people complain about not enough business and then they complain about being too busy. They complain about traffic, airport travel, not having enough time to do this or that. I simply do not get it. You are alive and most likely in good health, what is it that you find to complain about?

By now you know I came to this country with nothing, if I lose everything I have now but have my wife and my children, I'll be ok. I can start over anywhere on this planet. It helped me to never be attached to work and allowed me to go with the flow, no matter the ups and downs. This is not an outlook many folks share. I get it. It is easy to fall into the victim mentality.

Someone got a raise and you did not, you complain. Someone got leads handed out to them and you did not get any this time, you complain. Someone got a promotion ahead of you, you complain. Someone got a company trip and you did not, you complain. Company is changing things you complain; company is not changing things you complain. Right? Well, stop it. Go with a flow and if you truly feel overlooked and bypassed, well look in the mirror first, then if there is nothing wrong – get out of there.

Stop being miserable and move out! That's what complaining really place you in – the state of misery. It is time to relocate. When everyone around you complains and you are not, your co-workers might think you are a butt kisser or crazy. Here is a thing – it does not matter what they think, what matters is what the person who signs your checks think. So stop complaining and become thankful you have a job and you can provide for your living.

When I worked for a large automotive group, they went through four major changes – restructuring the entire processes, departments, pay plans, people's jobs, etc. This is all in the period of nine years. I handled it and never complained. This is one of the reasons promotions came to me – most of the complainers left the organization. This created vacuum and I was given plenty of opportunities to grow and benefit financially. An interesting thing happened later, many of the complainers came back. Now, in the spirit of full disclosure, when the fifth change began – it was too much for me to handle, and I left without complaining.

<u>Number five – bring more value than is expected from you.</u>

Always, do more than is expected from you. Remember the ones who say, *this is not part of my job? They don't pay me enough to do this. Or why am I always stuck doing this?* Well, those comments usually accompany number four – complainers. Also, these comments will rarely get you into a promotion situation.

Guess what? If you keep saying they don't pay you enough, they will always do that. Instead, step up to the plate and dish more than asked. As a matter of fact, start to do more. *I'm all done boss, what else can I do for you?*

Don't shy away from doing some manual labor even around the office. When you exceed their expectations you will be noticed. Now, let me clarify, do it with a genuine motive. You genuinely want to help and be a team player and not some career/advancement-seeking jerk who steps over everyone to get where he she wants to get. Do more because it is the right thing to do. Here is one of my principles – *I will always bring more value into the situation than is expected from me.* I will not ask for a raise. I will earn it because I bring so much value that my employer goes out of his way to take care of me.

One time I was doing some free training for a dealership and the dealer asked me why was I doing this?

"I'd like to bring value first and I know that my compensation will come from someone, it might not be from you, it most likely be from another source, but it will come."

Now I may have been stupid and should have asked her to pay me for it, but I did not. I was sowing good will and it came to me much later.

Number six – take ownership.

This one is hard for some people. Treat your position as if you owned the business you work at. Think about it. If your name was on the building, what would be different? Would you go by the piece of trash on the ground? Would you turn the lights off when you leave the office? Would you treat property with care? Copy machine anyone? Would you think twice before blurting out something out of line? Would you have more pep in your walk when you approach a customer? Would you make good on those promises you made? I can go on and on. It is easy just to treat your job like a job – I just spend 40 hours there. But if it was your own business would you treat it different? Look if the someone can trust you with their checkbook usually it is because you treat it as if it was your own. Believe me you will get noticed.

Taking ownership is not just about treating your workplace as if you owned it. It is also about taking ownership of issues and problems that you might be surrounded by. In their book "Extreme Ownership", two Navy SEAL officers, Jocko Willink and Leif Babin, speak about the way leaders in the Navy take ownership of their team's problems and mishaps. They own the problem even though they had no direct impact or involvement in those situations. If it happened on their watch they own it. These are great example of how you can own issues from small to big. If you do that, you will get noticed.

Number seven – Produce results.

Sales it is all about results. And in business producing results is all that really matters. Your contribution to your company's bottom line will determine the velocity of your promotion and amount of your reward. Nothing speaks louder than the cash register. As you are raining in profits and your company grows, so will you. What you do now must be with one goal in mind get results and allow your results to speak for themselves.

Out-work your co-workers, out-hustle your competition, place yourself in the top tier of whatever you do. When you do this - the opportunity will come. Show you are great at little things and big things will be given to you. If you can handle closing a small account and generating small revenue for your company, believe me the big ones will come your way. Of course your results are big reflection of what your skills are and what you bring to the table. So, results are crucial in positioning yourself. **Become a rainmaker and watch your career take off.**

Finally, Number 7.5 – live so no one can say anything bad about you.

Hey, I do know you cannot please everyone. That is not what I'm advocating. What I am saying is – do everything with class, so even the competition is baffled. There always will be plenty of hater around. They may hate you inside their own head, but give them no reason to say anything bad about you. Look I had a privilege to work for a company with 850 employees. In my industry it was considered a mid-size operation. Because I was a corporate trainer I personally knew just about every one of those employees. You can go back and ask every one of them about me, you will get nothing but positive feedback. I gave them no reason to say anything bad about me. Did we disagree about things? Oh, yes we did, but they still respected me.

Hey, no one is perfect we all make mistakes and we all can have issues with people. When you treat everyone around you with respect and dignity you will position yourself for opportunities.

Here is a recap to position yourself for growth follow these 7.5 things:

#1 show up on time,

#2 be prepared,

#3 set goals,

#4 never complain,

#5 bring more value than is expected from you,

#6 treat it as if you own it,

#7 produce massive results and

#7.5 live so no one can say anything bad about you.

MY TAKEAWAYS:

I will start _____
_____
_____
_____
_____
_____
_____
_____
_____
_____

I will stop _____
_____
_____
_____
_____
_____
_____
_____
_____
_____

5 STEPS TO A PAY RAISE.

CHAPTER 9

The other day I read a post about $250K being new $100K. Making $100K does not seem like a lot nowadays. I have been fortunate to be well above this mark during the last 10 years or so. And I can tell you that this might be true. The average household income in USA is $52K and less than 30% earn that. For the longest time earning $100K was a dream of many sales professionals. This is still possible of course, but one would have to place their sights higher.

The above mentioned post says that $250K is more like the $100K of 10-15 years ago. Of course with inflation, cost of living things can get tighter and tighter. More income does make life easier. I mean you can give more to charity, you can help people more, you can provide for your family with more, what motivates you? And what are you doing to earn more?

Long time ago when talking about income, the business philosopher Jim Rohn, said that one cannot make money – Federal Reserve does that – you and I can earn money. I know it is play on words and for many people this may seem like semantics, but there is a lot of truth in it. I think another time Jim said – Your pay raise will become effective when you are. There is so much wisdom in those statements. And even though we might get it, but how do we actually get to a pay raise? Over the years I found several ways that work to get a raise you desire. Here are the five steps to getting to your next pay level.

Number ONE – do more than you are asked to do.

Giving more of your time and energy at work is super important. You want to stand out? Work. The mediocrity is such a common thing in the work force nowadays. There is a sense of entitlement – *They don't pay me enough, or this is not my responsibility* – thinking like this will not get you far. Showing up on time and giving more than you were required to do will be a great first step to getting a pay raise. Look, if you are in sales chances are you are getting paid commissions in addition to some base pay. Even if you are on straight 100% commissions you can still do more than it is required of you. Look pay raise will come weather it is through your base pay going up or you get more business because you give more – it will happen.

Number TWO – work your pay plan.

Here is the thing – every great sales person I ever met worked his/her pay plan. They understood what and how it works. Your pay plan should be your job description and if this is the case you working your pay plan simply means you are working as your job description outlines. This is important piece of information. Be smart about it. Working your pay plan also means you maximize every opportunity it provides you. If you get paid on volume – sell volume. If you get paid on gross profit you generate – then plan accordingly maximize profitability. What is your pay plan? Do you understand it? I mean I have seen some confusing almost contradicting – schizophrenic pay plans and they are hard to follow. Hopefully you have an easy to follow pay plan that will reward you with more opportunity to earn more. Focus on activities that will maximize your pay and then maximize those activities.

Number THREE – be a team player.

Look sales is dog-eat-dog world. But what I found is when you help people around you to be successful, it will rub off on you. You will get helped when needed as well. I worked in environments where you were left alone with no help and quite frankly it felt like a hostile environment. The entire culture was anti-social. Through that though I was still able to connect with others and assist them in their sales. That translated into more opportunities for me. Then I worked in cultures where everyone is pitching in and it does not matter "who's customer" it is, it is everybody's customer type of culture and approach. This may not seem like a key to getting a pay raise – but it is. When you help other you will get noticed. Warning, make sure you do this not to get noticed but really help your team.

Number FOUR – become indispensable by closing deals.

When you close deals at a rate higher than anyone else in the company or at least your production is in the top 10% you are positioning yourself for a raise. When you are hard to replace it gives you leverage. This one is an interesting one, since when you are a top notch closer your status with the company grows and you get to the top tier of your pay scale. Getting this done is not easy but that is your goal.

Chances are success in your company is determined by production levels. The leverage you get by getting there is awesome. I have been fortunate to be part of winning teams and be one of the top producers. Make it your goal!!!

Number FIVE – ask for it.

When you have done everything you can sometimes all you need to do is ask for a pay raise. I have seen people ask for a raise when they have not done the first four things I mentioned. This gives them little to no leverage and quite frankly annoys the boss. I had people ask me for a raise when I was a General Manager of a large dealership. Realize this, because you have more bills does not mean your boss is responsible for it. Your bills are your problem. Asking for a raise can backfire on you. The conventional logic tells you the best times to do that is during or right after your job review. I found the best time is when you perform beyond expectations and bring massive value.

Here is one thing to remember, you never want to hold your employer hostage with your pay. I mean you do not want to threaten them in any way – you pay or else I leave. This is never a good strategy and it is right down stupid. You will not generate much good will from your boss.

Here is a recap the five things you can do to get a raise:

    1. Do more than asked

    2. Work your pay plan

    3. Be a team player

    4. Close deals – be a top producer

    5. Ask for it

MY TAKEAWAYS:

I will start _____

_____
_____
_____
_____
_____
_____
_____
_____
_____
_____
_____

I will stop _____

_____
_____
_____
_____
_____
_____
_____
_____
_____
_____
_____
_____
_____

GET YOUR SALES CAREER ON TRACK.

CHAPTER 10

Let's look at your job in sales. I have been involved in sales from a very young age. My first real sale job was selling electronics at Sears. It was a part time gig while I was in college. This was in mid-90s and Sears had little to no competition. I worked through college in sales and then during my grad school for a short time as well. After finishing grad school and getting a degree in counseling, I could not find a position in the field. I decided to get into sales again. This time it was car sales. I know, right? Master degree and car sales? Really? Well, I wanted to earn some money and this was an option. When I got into this field I thought it would be temporary, because my ideal job was out there somewhere.

For the first two years I did well, but I still wanted to find that perfect job. I moved to Minnesota to join friend's business and grow. It did not pan out and after six months I went back to car sales. Again I thought it was temporary. I was still looking for this perfect job. In my mind I did not want to settle for career in sales. Car sales on top of that. I listen to the sales trainer who said that if you were in car sales you were sitting on the best financial opportunity, if you work smart. I gave it a little more thought and followed his advice. Up until that time I was working but not working smart. I guess I was like a flip phone not a smart one. I flipped back and forth in and out of the business. This was happening daily – back and forth.

One day I was committed to the business then the other day I would look for wanted ads. One foot in one foot out. Sound familiar? You may experience the same. I think my ADD was getting in the middle of it. Oh, look a squirrel. This back and forth interfered with my mindset and messed up my sales flow.

You might know what I'm talking about. You plan to focus on your activity, but then you get frustrated with little to no outcome and shift your attention to something else, this will disrupt your original activity and you lose interest towards it all together. It's like a cycle that get you into a trap and it is hard to get out.

Sometimes, going to work is not fun. You force yourself to drive there. Your days become long. You lose interest in doing your activities. Phone calls are a drag, talking to clients is a drag. You slowly become disengaged and your results show it. There really two outcomes – you must quit or you change your outlook.

Here what happened to me. I began to re-evaluate my approach to my work. You see I really was never taught organizational skills for sales position. All this time I just relied on the hope strategy. I hoped customers would show up, I hoped I was prepared for the presentation. I hoped I knew enough and do enough to close the deal.

There was no structure to my daily activities. 99% of the time I just winged it. The wing it approach may work for some, some of the time as it did for me. The problem with this approach was, sales were not fun, because I did not see great results I expected. Once I realized there is more to sales world than just wondering around and waiting for things to happen, I began to approach it more strategically. Below are **three steps** to get your sales career into an overdrive.

Number one – set goals.

You read about this already. I'm going to be a broken record. In my experience over ninety percent of sales people do not set real goals. I mean if you ask them they will tell you *"oh I have a goal. I want to sell xx amount of whatever they are selling"* I have been to many sales meetings where goals are supposedly set – I call them the blue sky meetings. Sales people set unrealistic goals – results that they have never been able even come close to. I know I know you want to shoot for the stars and so forth, but let me tell you, if you have never got on the top of a small hill how are you going to clime an Everest. It is great to have a goal of reaching a summit on Everest, but you don't do it in your first month of mountain climbing.

SO let's get to the hill first and be strategic enough to reach your ultimate goal. Don't blue sky yourself but establish realistic and achievable goals. By the way goals must also be set for your activities. This is one of thing that made me fall in love with my work. I began tracking my activities and focusing on those instead of the end result – the sale. The second thing I did is wrote my goal on paper. People have their goals inside their head, but it is out of side out of mind situation. You cannot see what's inside your head. Goals must be visual. Write them out on a piece of paper, on a card on your phone screen shot, everywhere you are you must see it. Post it in your house have it in your car. I have cards in my car with my goals.

What to do with goals – write them down, carry them with you, create activities goals, make your immediate goals realistic and achievable, and set your big and scary goals as well. Those big goals will push you hard as well. Began climbing your hills and mountains or running a race, whatever analogy you want to use.

Number two – act.

The second thing that got me going is action. It is so easy just sit and talk about what you are going to do, but it is actually much harder to just do it. Nike! Hey one of my bosses used to call me – **GID – get it done** – this was way before Larry the Cable guy was around. I adopted that name and carried with pride telling people my middle name was GID – get it done baby!

Actions is what will energize you and surprise you as well. The biggest thing that stops people from executing their plan is fear. Fear of failure, fear of rejection, fear of success, fear of the unknown – what will happen when I pick up the phone and call that prospect? What's the worst thing that could happen? They might hang up! OK can you survive that? When fear paralyzes you it usually comes in the form of procrastination or laziness. Get over your fears and make things happen! Getting things done require hustle. You must move you must hustle.

Progress requires action – if you don't hustle don't plan to see great results. Good things do come to those who go and get things done. Listen – no one will make things happen for you. If it is to be it is up to me. Right? Stop procrastinating. There never be a perfect time perfect opportunity – you make time perfect and make opportunity perfect.

Don't wait for the right climate – create your own climate GET THINGS DONE!!!

Number three – track your progress.

My biggest opportunities came when I was prepared for them. I planned, I acted and I tracked things. Here is the thing, when you track your progress you are exposing yourself daily to where you are in relationship to your goal. This forces and motivates you to keep on taking more action to be on par or exceed your goal. Keeping track of your activities and results daily helps you stay focus on your goals. It is so easy to get distracted and lose focus. This is when your mind began to wonder off into the left field and next thing you know you hate your job because you don't or can't get any results.

You cannot be half committed to your profession as a sales person. You either in or out. When you are half way into sales you get half the results, you lose your passion about your industry and next thing you know you looking at the wanted ads whether by choice or not. Get your sales grove on! Start or keep setting goals but with a new approach. Next take action! Nothing bad will happen when you ask for an order. I have not seen anyone reach over the table and slap a sales person when they asked for an order. So get over your fears and sell! Finally, get your grove on, with tracking your progress. No one is responsible for your success – you are. Now go make it happen – Plan, Act and Track!

MY TAKEAWAYS:

I will start _____

_____
_____
_____
_____
_____
_____
_____
_____
_____
_____

I will stop _____

_____
_____
_____
_____
_____
_____
_____
_____
_____
_____
_____

BECOMING A
STONE-COLD SELLER.

The definition of being "stone-cold" implies being complete or total. This makes the path of becoming a stone-cold seller not an easy one. Being a complete salesperson is in a way similar to chasing perfection. It was the great Vince Lombardi who said: ***"Perfection is not attainable, but if we chase perfection we can catch excellence."*** This is a great aspiration, and the road to excellence is an admirable one.

There is no one way to get there. You are the sum-total of all your life experiences up to this point. In other words, the road you traveled up to this point influenced who you are right now. Good, bad or indifferent you are who you are because of the choices you made in the past. Here is what's great about life, you can change your course and improve your chances on becoming better at anything you do. It takes a simple choice or series of choices. I realize, sometimes it may not be as simple as this, but don't over complicate things – no one can make choices for you. You can control the direction you want to go. Let's review what will bulletproof your sales career in an unbeatable way:

1. making a commitment to yourself and those who depend on you - make a decision and get both feet into your sales career.
2. pay attention to those you surround yourself with, are they lifting you up or dragging you down, both in production and attitudes.
3. work on your sales muscle, read, learn and keep investing into sales training.
4. learn to recognize what lowers sales resistance and raise buyer curiosity.
5. master how to outpace your competition by becoming both a great hunter and farmer.
6. work on improving your career by positioning yourself for promotion and a pay raise.
7. finally keep your career on track by setting aggressive goals, executing your plan and tracking your progress.

It is time for you to stop waiting for your sales environment to improve. No one is going to change things for you. You must create your own environment! This country is great because people here are great at implementing things. Follow what the French guy in the first chapter's story said, ***stop strategizing, start doing!***

MY TAKEAWAYS:

I will start _____

_____

I will stop _____

_____

About the Author

Tony began his sales career at the age of fourteen on the streets of a large city in the former Soviet Union, where he learned the hustle of the black market. At eighteen he came to the USA to pursue an American Dream with only $50 in his pocket and half-full suitcase.

He had a successful career in the retail automotive business. His experiences included finance, sales management and director of training for an organization with 1000 employees. As a general manager of a large dealership, he led the team of 135 employees to become a top 100 Toyota dealership in US. Since 2011 Tony has been working with businesses coaching, consulting and training leadership and sales teams. His expertise is helping businesses create a sales-driven culture and drive better results through process improvement. Tony practices what he teaches, he is a sales leader for his company, generating over $2million in residual income working within B2B environment. His clients include, numerous automotive dealerships, real estate teams, Hyundai, Lexus and J.D. Power.

With over 600 presentations and 2500 hours platform training Tony is a sought after speaker and trainer. He is one of 750 speakers in the world to earn a prestigious designation of a Certified Speaking Professional™ by National Speakers Association. He is a frequent speaker at Auto Industry conferences and his articles are published in various publications. His international work includes speaking and training in places like Korea, Portugal and UAE.

 atroussov@gmail.com

 @atroussov

 linkedin.com/in/ttroussov/

Made in the USA
Monee, IL
21 December 2020